EASY PIANO

ADELE

ISBN 978-1-4584-1321-5

HAL•LEONARD®
CORPORATION

7777 W. BLUEMOUND RD. P.O. BOX 13819 MILWAUKEE, WI 53213

Visit Hal Leonard Online at
www.halleonard.com

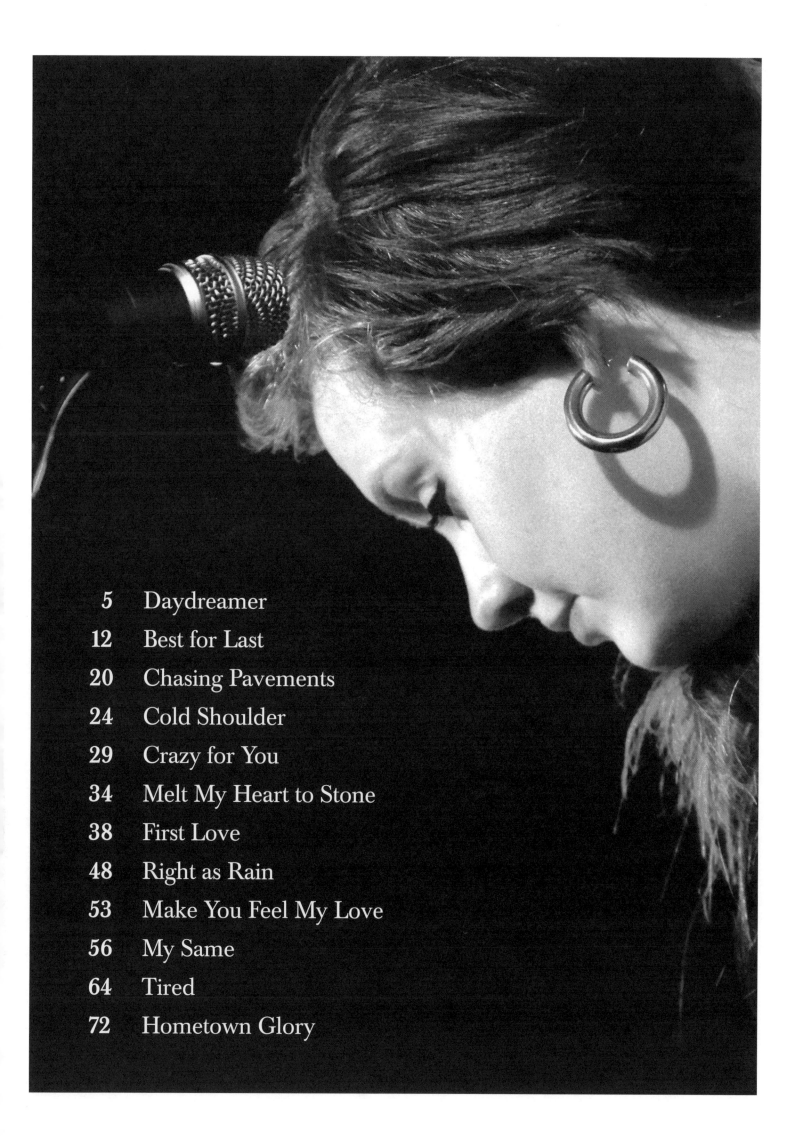

DAYDREAMER

Words and Music by
ADELE ADKINS

fig - ure be - fore.
Instrumental

A jaw __ drop -
Instrumental Ends Day - dream -

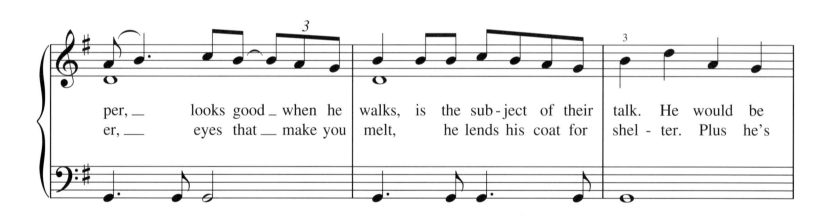

per, __ looks good __ when he walks, is the sub-ject of their talk. He would be
er, __ eyes that __ make you melt, he lends his coat for shel - ter. Plus he's

hard __ to __ chase, but good to catch and he could change the world with his
there __ for you when he should - n't be, but he stays all the same, waits for

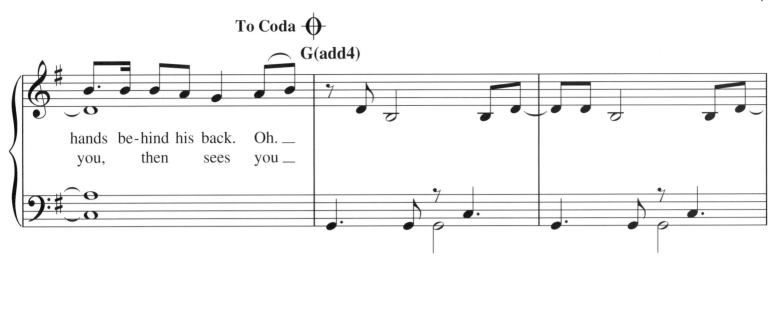

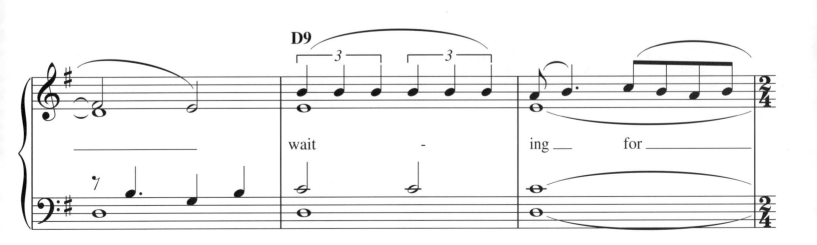

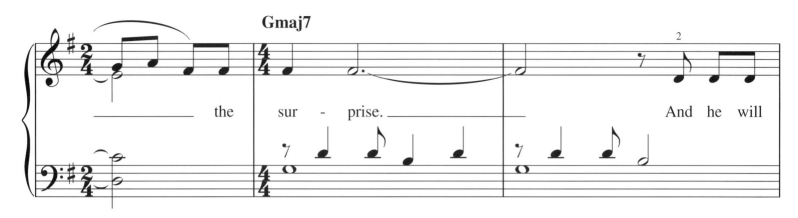

the sur - prise. _____ And he will

feel like he's been there for hours, _____

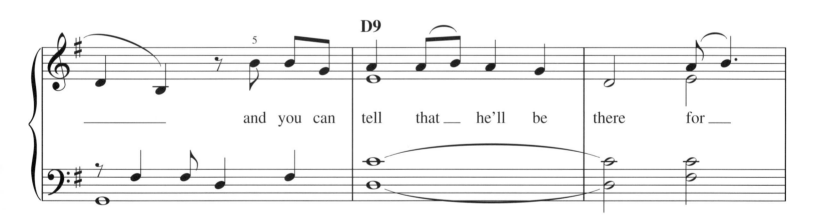

_____ and you can tell that __ he'll be there for __

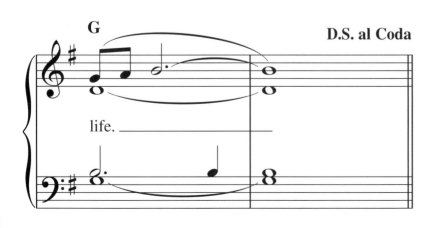

life. _____

D.S. al Coda

CODA

through.

There's no way I could de-

scribe him. What I've said is

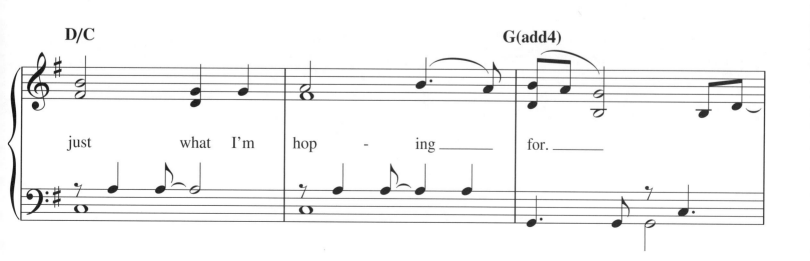

just what I'm hop - ing _____ for. _____

D9

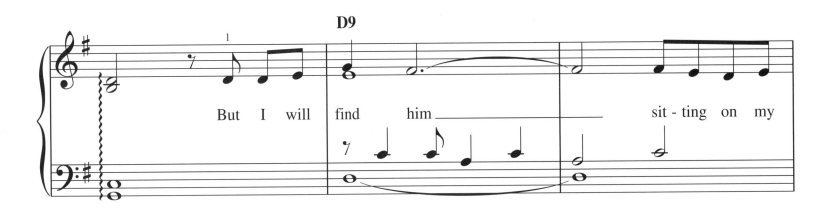

But I will find him _____ sit - ting on my

Gmaj7   **D9**

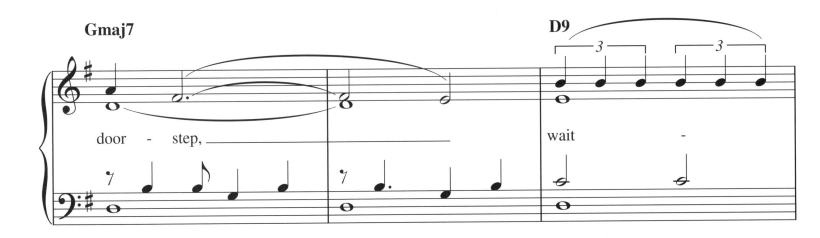

door - step, _____ wait -

Gmaj7

ing _____ for _____ a sur - prise. _____

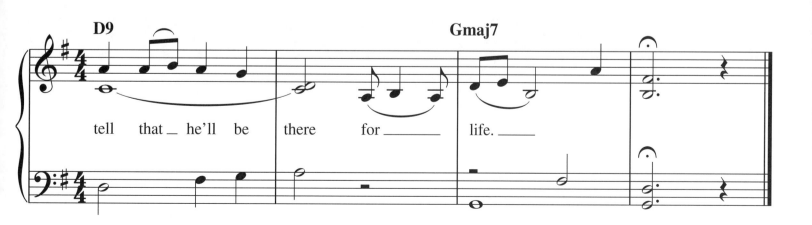

BEST FOR LAST

Words and Music by
ADELE ADKINS

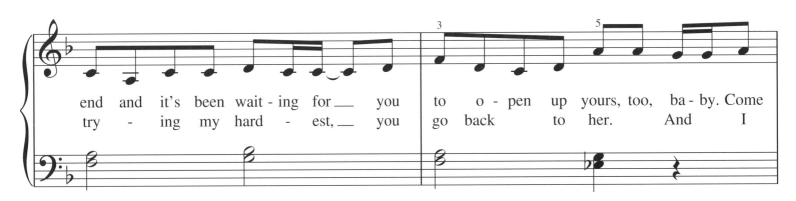

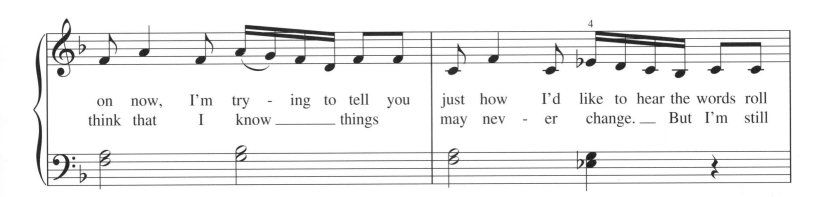

out of your mouth fi - nal - ly. Say that it's al - ways been me that's made you
hop - ing one day I _____ might hear you say... I make you

Moderately slow, in 2

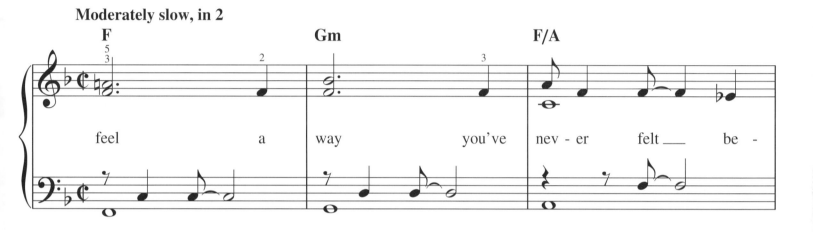

feel a way you've nev - er felt _____ be -

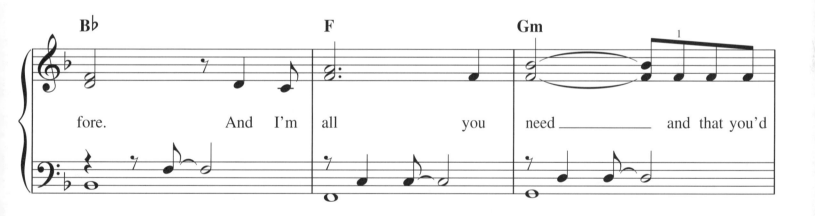

fore. And I'm all you need _____ and that you'd

nev - er want _ more. Then you'd say

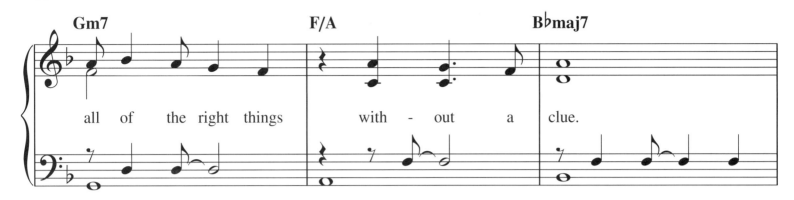

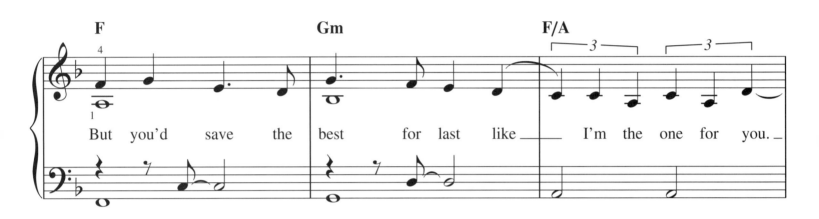

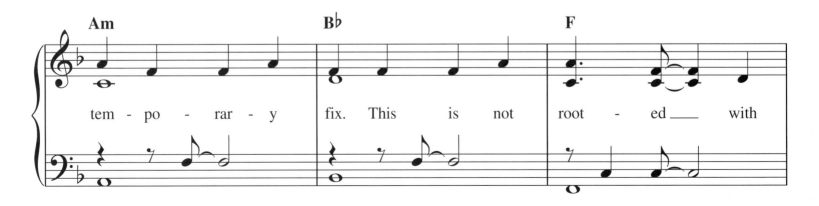

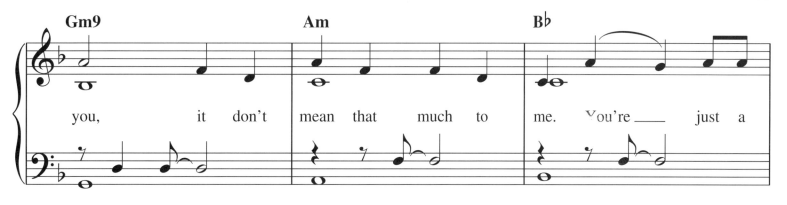

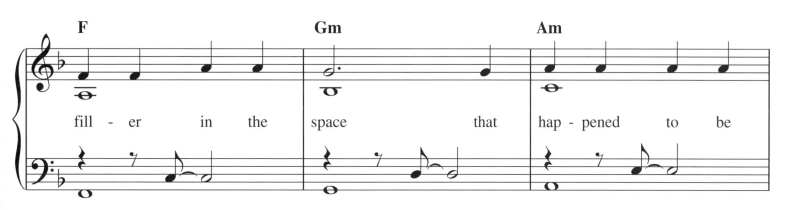

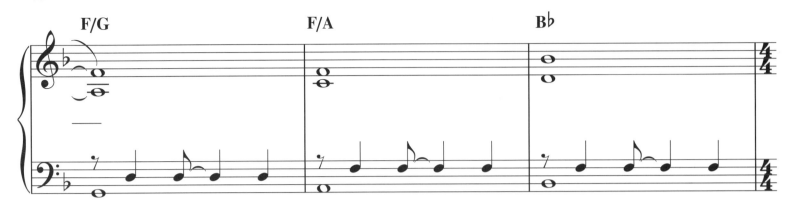

run - ning __ a - round. __ And I will do __ un -

til I __ find __ my - self with you and make you

feel a way you've nev - er felt __ be - fore. And be

all __ you need __ so that you nev - er want __ more. __ Then

you'd say all of the right things _ with - out _ a clue.

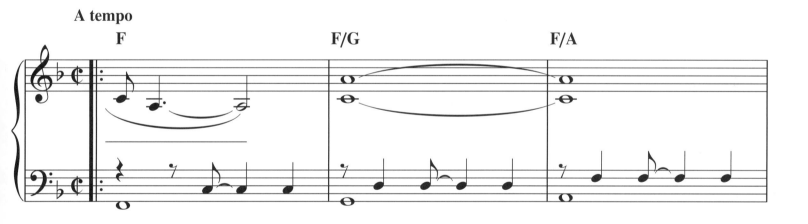

And you'll be the one for me and _ me the one for you. _ Yeah. _

A tempo

F   F/G   F/A

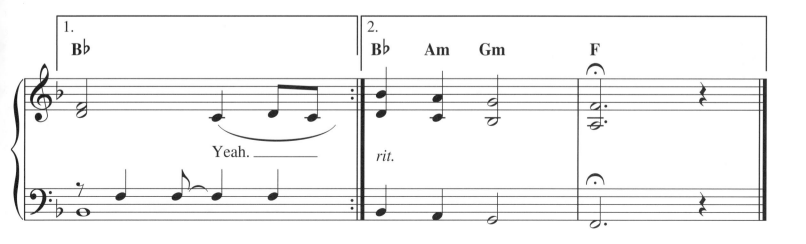

1.   B♭   2.   B♭   Am   Gm   F

Yeah. _____   *rit.*

CHASING PAVEMENTS

Words and Music by ADELE ADKINS
and FRANCIS EG WHITE

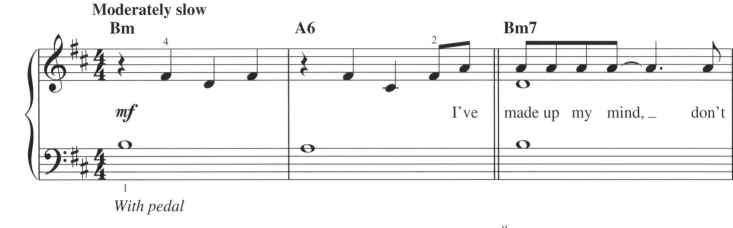

I've made up my mind, __ don't

need to think it o-ver. If I'm wrong, I am __ right, __ don't need to look no fur-ther. This ain't

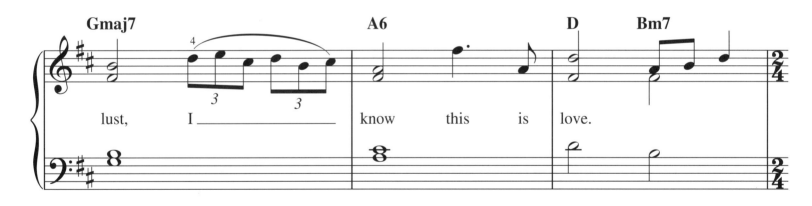

lust, I _____ know this is love.

But if I tell the world, __ I'll nev-er say e-nough, 'cause it was
build my-self up _____ and fly a-round in cir-cles, wait-ing

22

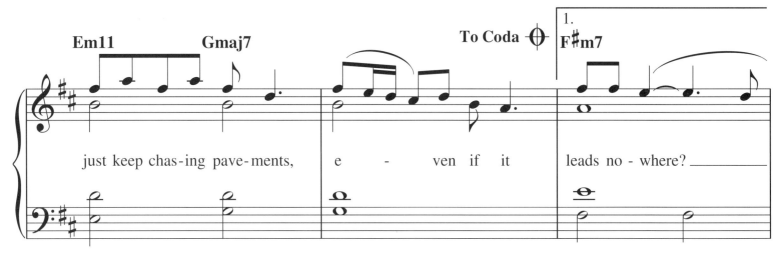

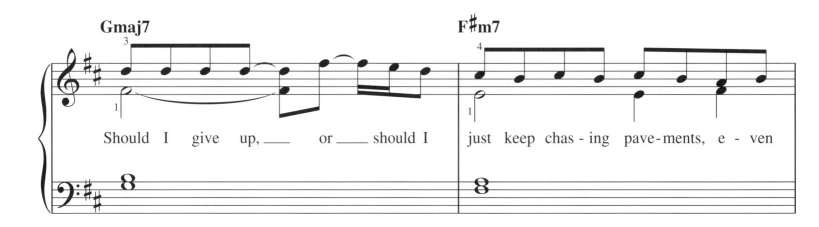

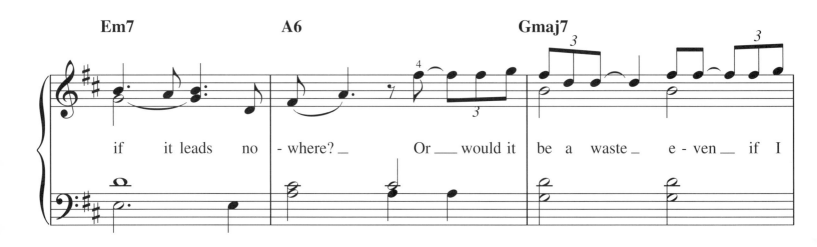

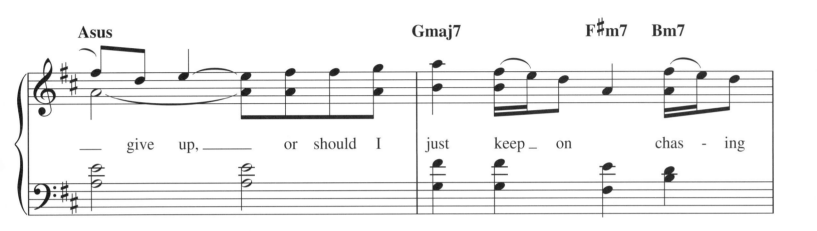

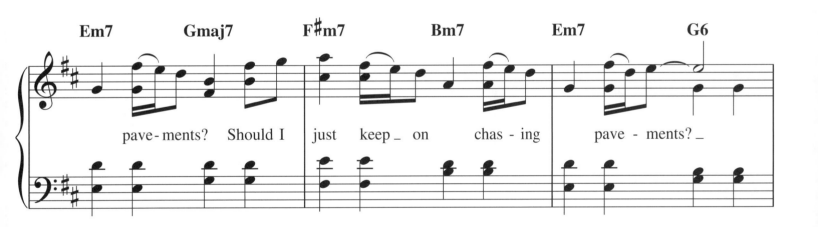

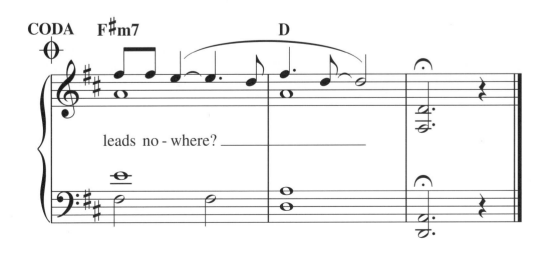

COLD SHOULDER

Words and Music by ADELE ADKINS
and SACHA SKARBEK

C   **G**   **C**

see   that look in   your   eyes, ___ the one that   shoots   me   each and ev -'ry
know   just how   you   feel. ___ I'm start-ing   to   find my-self feel-ing that way

G   **E/G♯**   **Am7**   **Em7**

time.   You   grace me with your cold   shoul -   der _____ when-ev - er
too, when   you

Am7   **Em**   **C**

you look at   me and wish I   was   her. __   You   show-er   me with words made of

G6   **G**   **Am7**   **B7**

knives   when-ev - er   you look at   me and wish I   was   her. _____

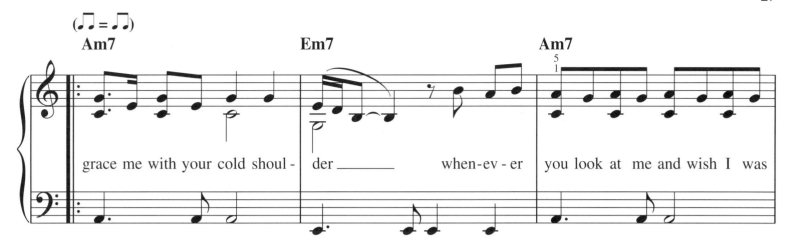

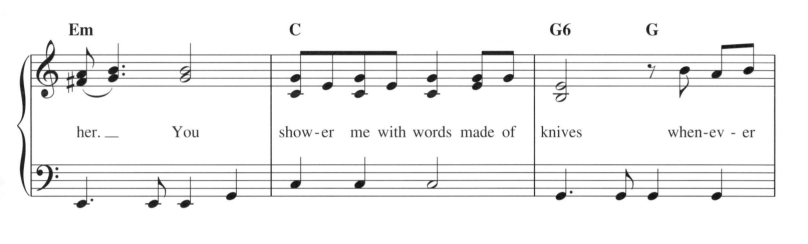

CRAZY FOR YOU

Words and Music by
ADELE ADKINS

am, ___ I'm ___ cra - zy ___ for you.
send ___ me spin - ning clos - er ___ to you.

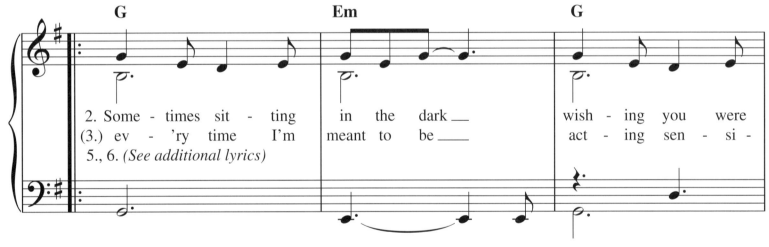

2. Some - times sit - ting in the dark ___ wish - ing you were
(3.) ev - 'ry time I'm meant to be ___ act - ing sen - si -
5., 6. *(See additional lyrics)*

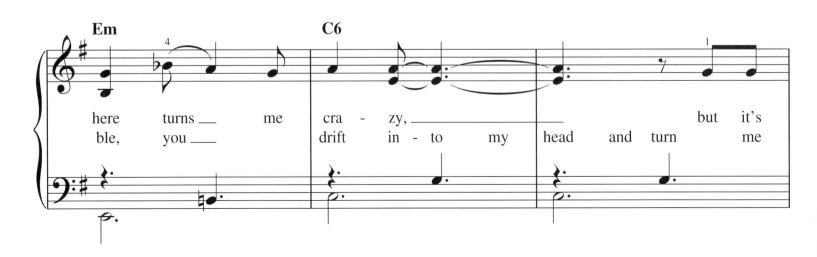

here turns ___ me cra - zy, ___ but it's
ble, you ___ drift in - to my head and turn me

Additional Lyrics

5. My, oh my, how my blood boils,
   It's sweetest for you.
   It strips me down bare
   And gets me into my favorite mood.

6. I keep on trying,
   I'm fighting these feelings away.
   But the more I do,
   The crazier I turn into.

MELT MY HEART TO STONE

Words and Music by ADELE ADKINS
and FRANCIS EG WHITE

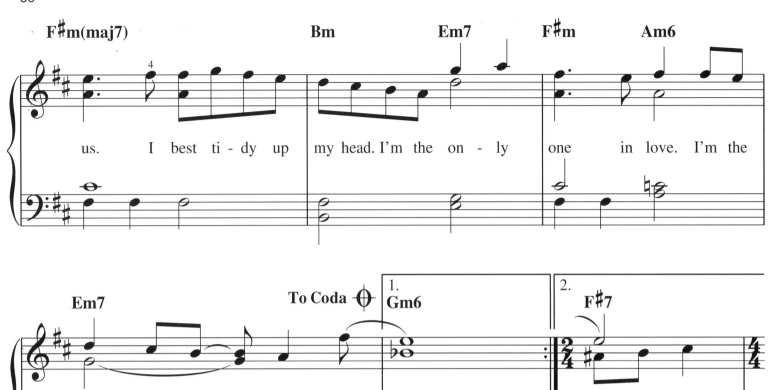

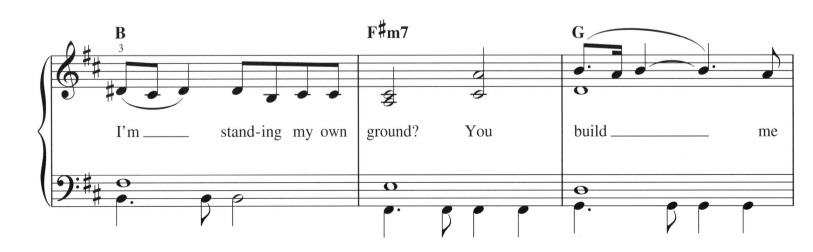

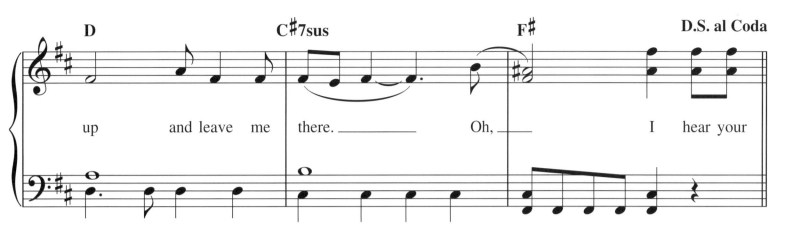

up and leave me there. _____ Oh, ___ I hear your

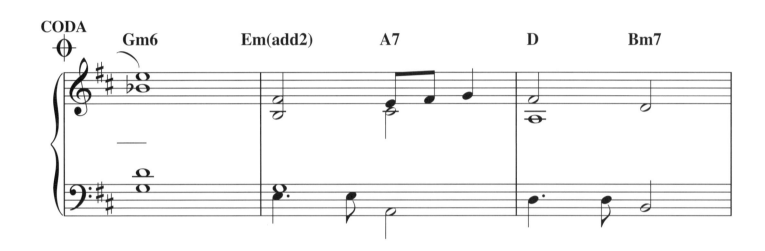

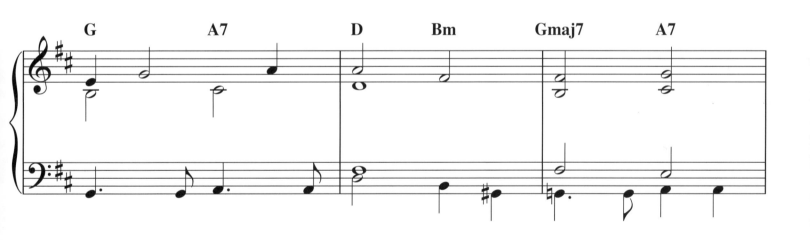

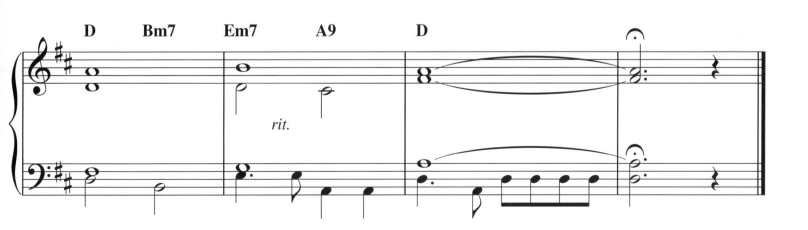

FIRST LOVE

Words and Music by
ADELE ADKINS

Waltz tempo, in 1

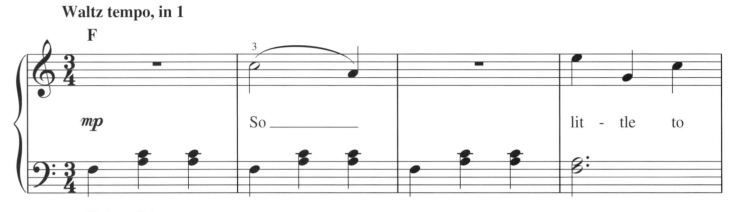

With pedal

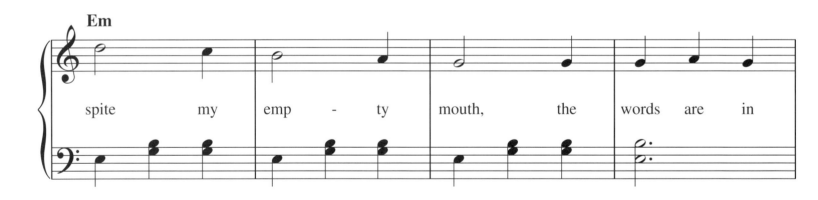

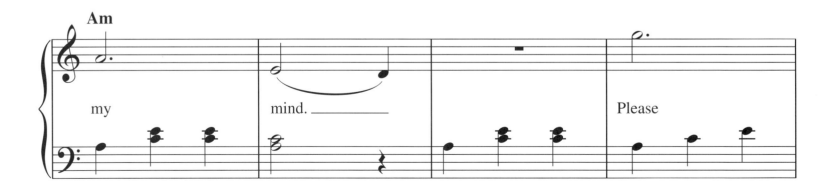

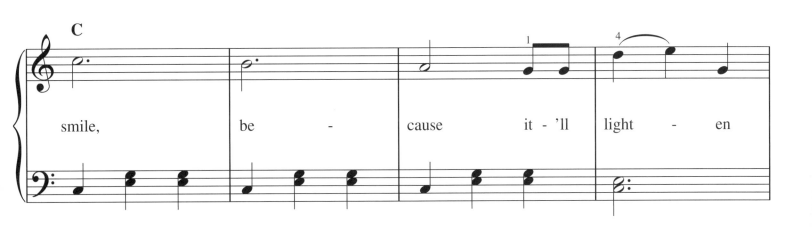

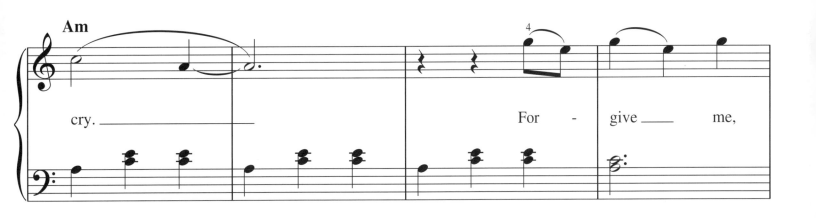

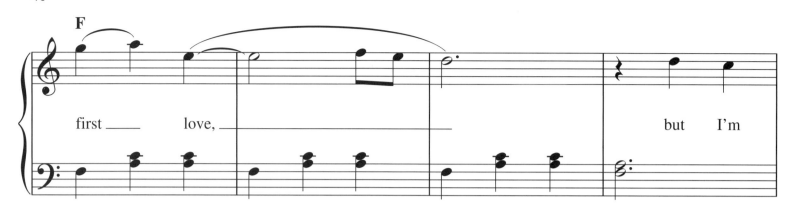

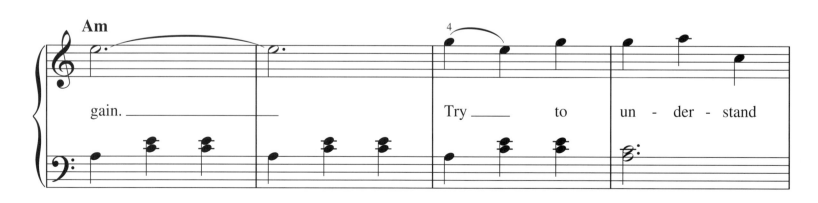

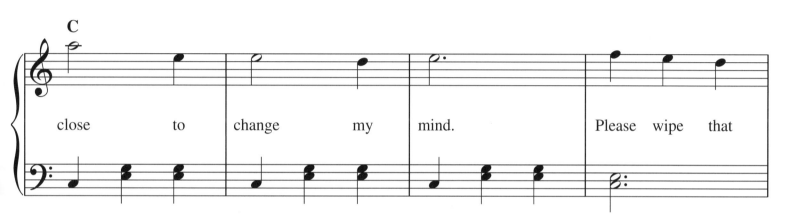

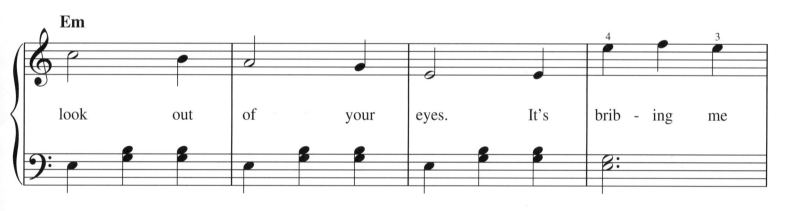

ply, _____ it's

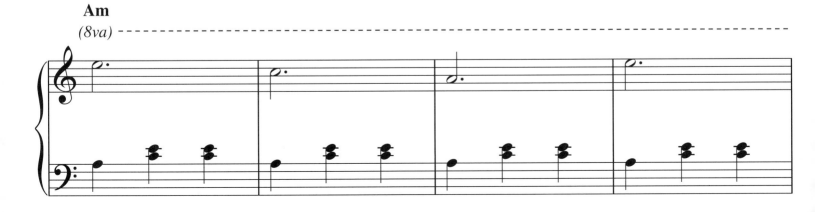

time. _____ *Both hands 8va* -------------------------

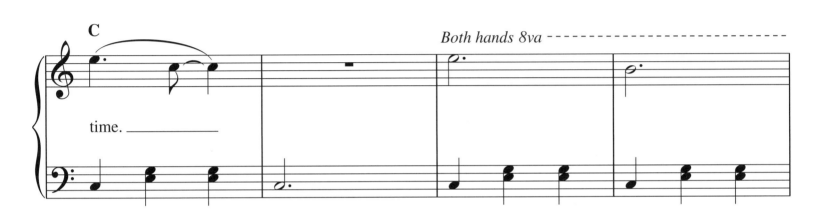

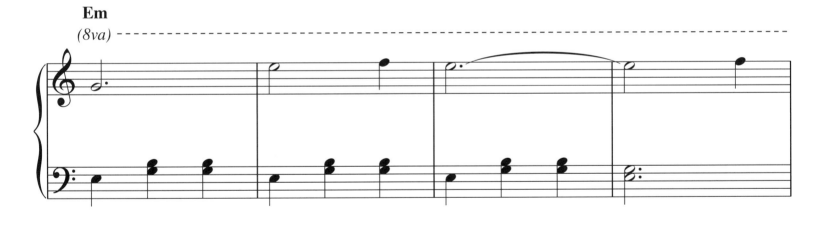

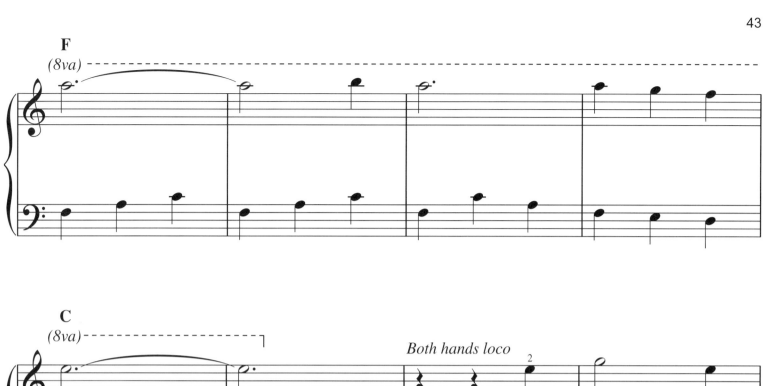

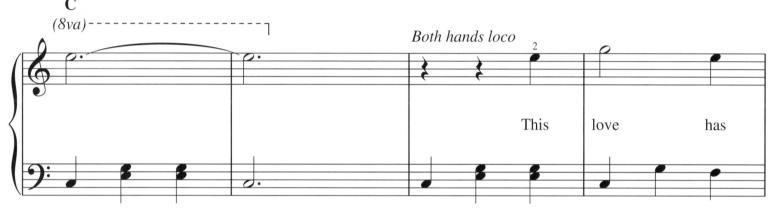

This love has

dried ___ up _____ and stayed be -

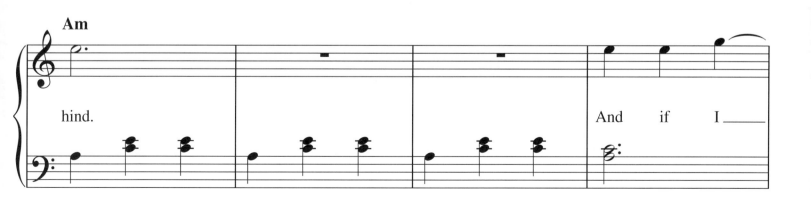

hind. And if I ____

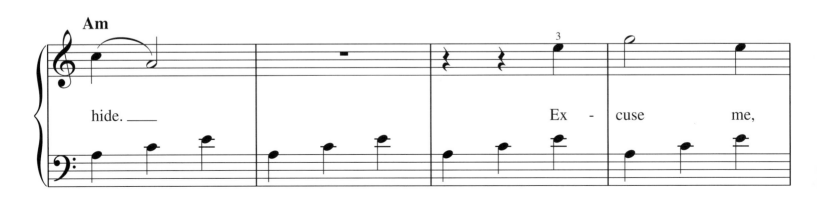

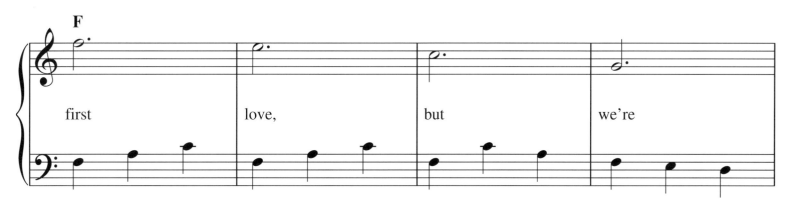

F first love, but we're

C through. I need to

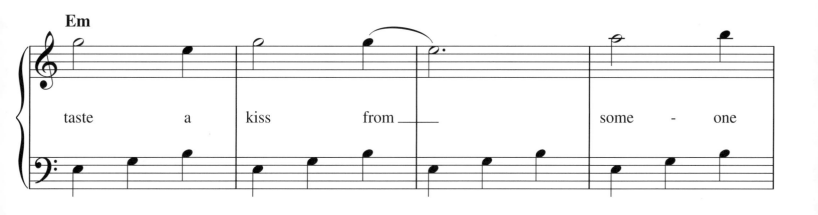

Em taste a kiss from some - one

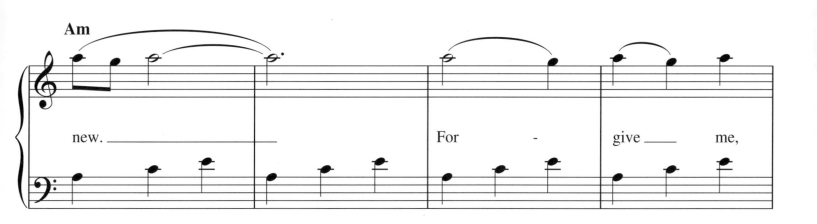

Am new. For - give me,

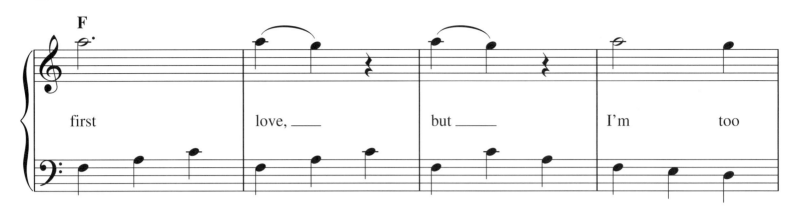

F

first love, ____ but ____ I'm too

C

tired. ____ I'm ____

Em

bored, to say the least, and ____ I lack de-

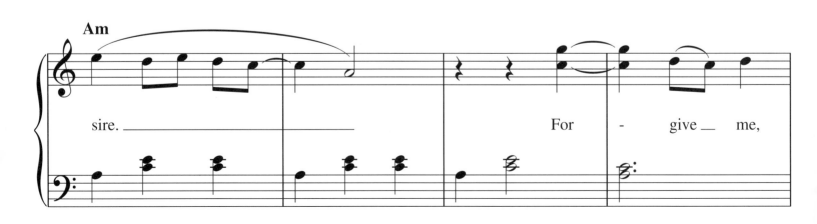

Am

sire. ____ For - give ___ me,

first _____ love. _____ For - give me,

first _____ love. _____ For - give me,

first love. _____ *dim. e rit. al fine* For - give me,

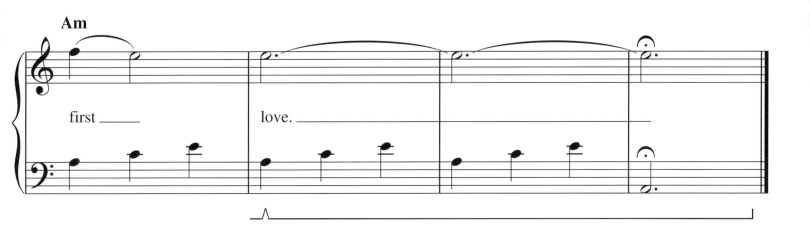

first _____ love. _____

RIGHT AS RAIN

Words and Music by ADELE ADKINS,
LEON MICHELS, JEFF SILVERMAN,
CLAY HOLLEY and NICK MOVSHON

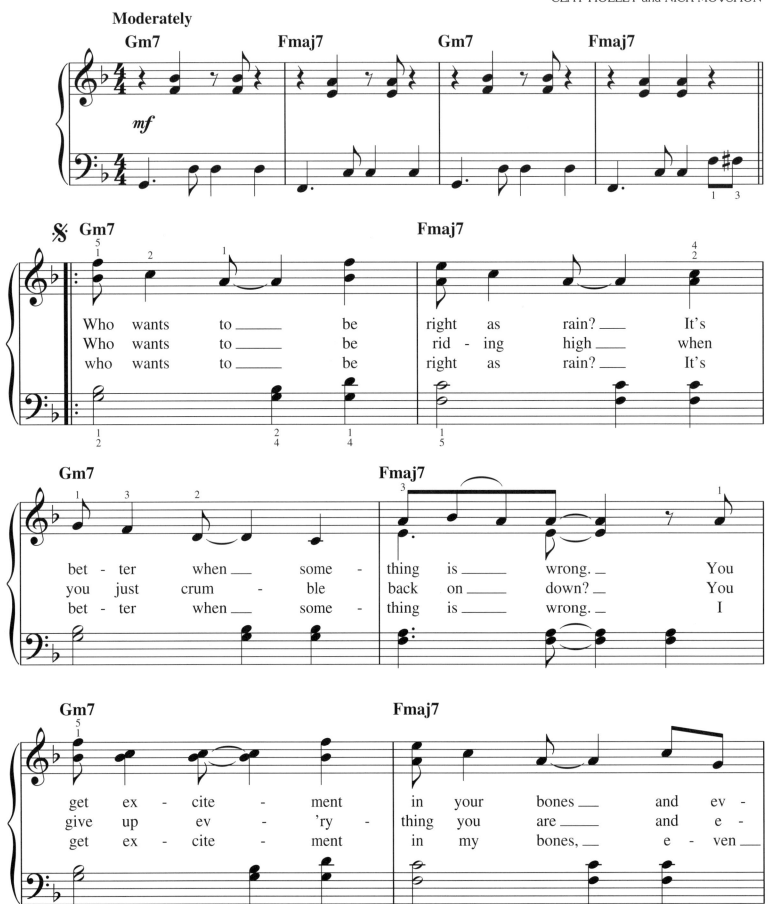

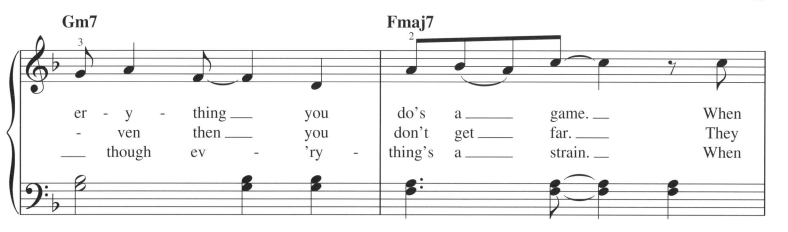

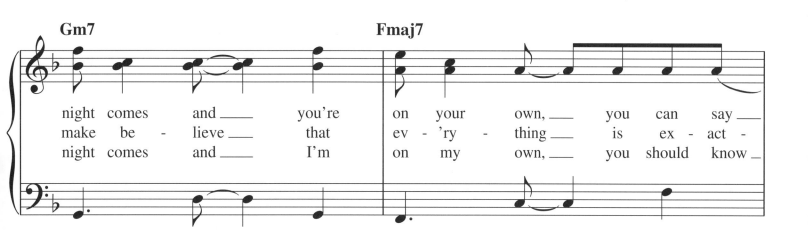

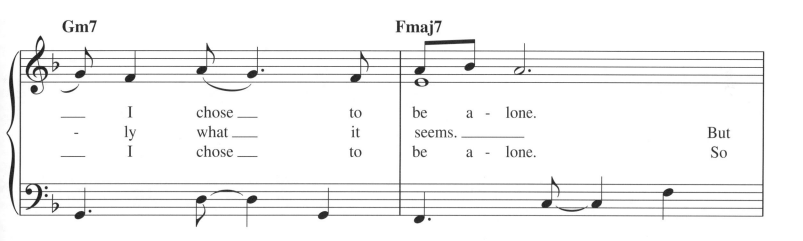

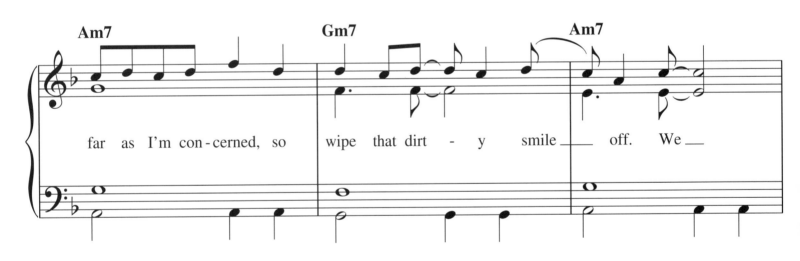

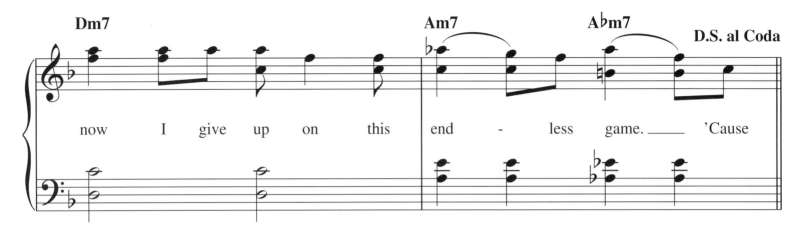

now I give up on this end - less game. _____ 'Cause

love. _____ Yeah, _____

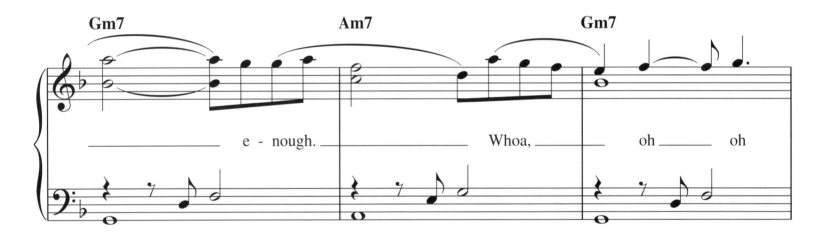

_____ e - nough. _____ Whoa, _____ oh _____ oh

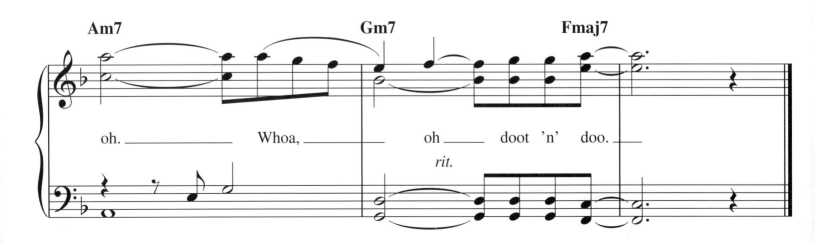

oh. _____ Whoa, _____ oh _____ doot 'n' doo. _____

MAKE YOU FEEL MY LOVE

Words and Music by
BOB DYLAN

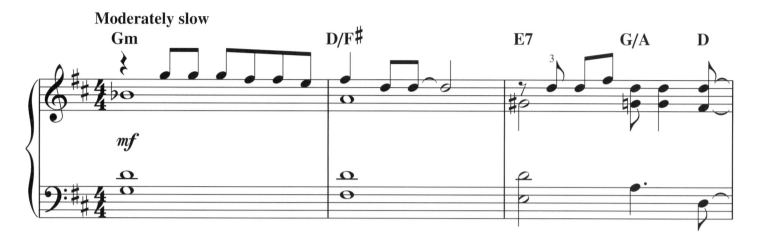

When the rain is blow-ing in your face, _
When the eve-ning shat-ters and the stars ap - pear, _

and the whole world is on your case, _ I could of - fer you a
and there is no one there to dry your tears, _ I could hold you for a

I'd go hun-gry, I'd go black and blue, _ I'd go crawl-ing down the
I could make you hap - py, make your dreams come true, _ noth-ing that _ I _

av - e - nue. _ Know there's noth-ing that I would-n't do _
would-n't do. _ Go to the ends of the earth for you _

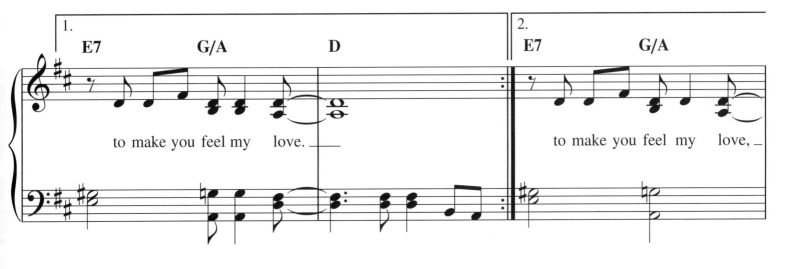

1.
to make you feel my love. _

2.
to make you feel my love, _

_ to make you feel my love. _

rit.

MY SAME

Words and Music by
ADELE ADKINS

With motion

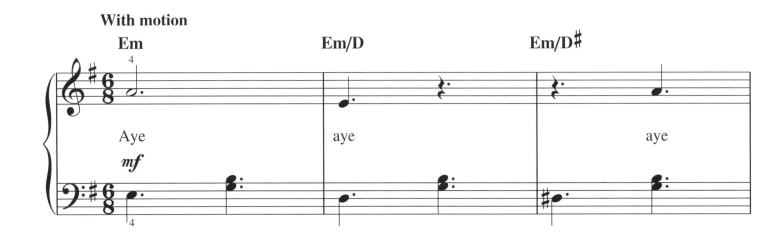

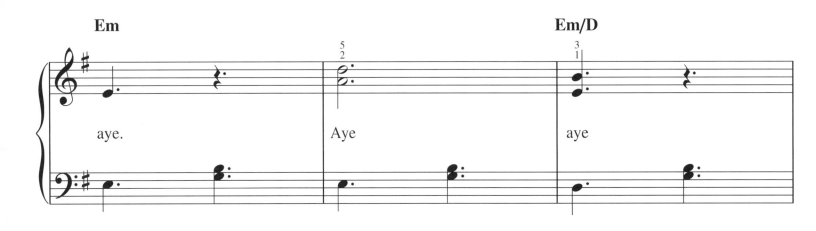

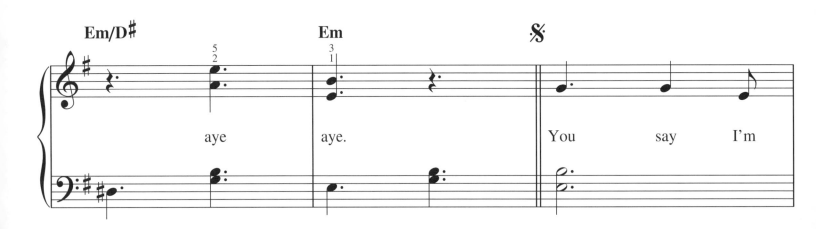

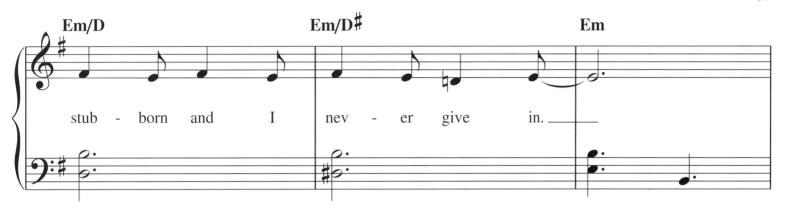

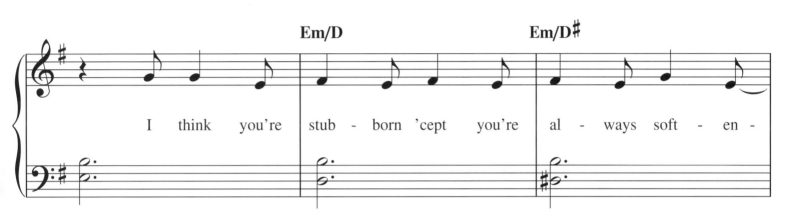

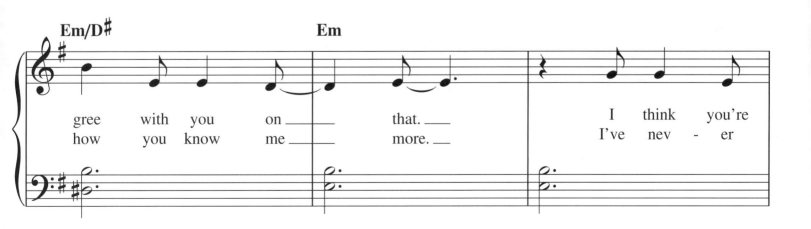

58

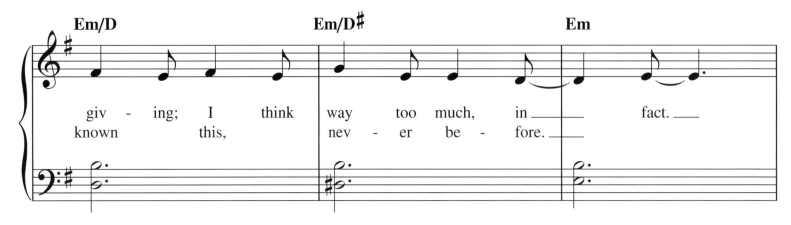

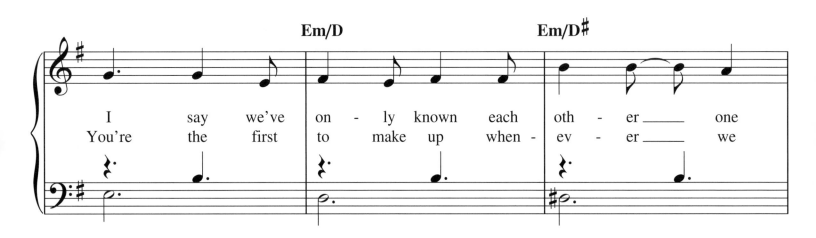

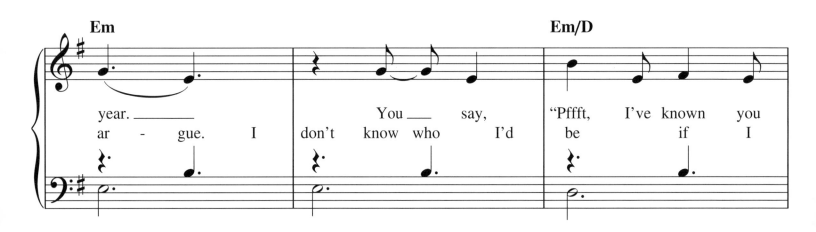

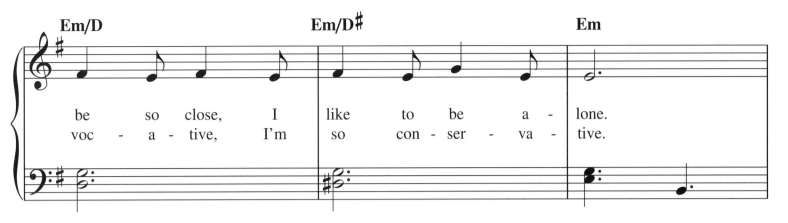

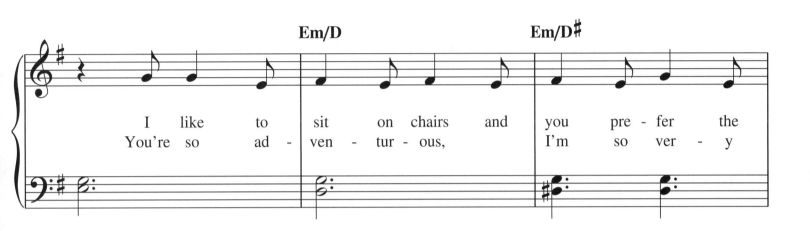

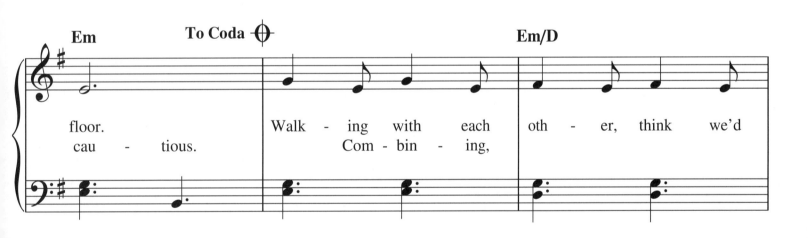

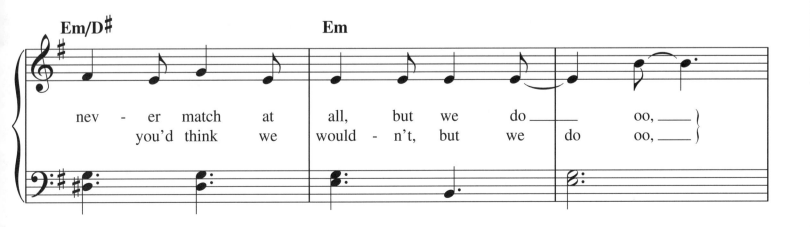

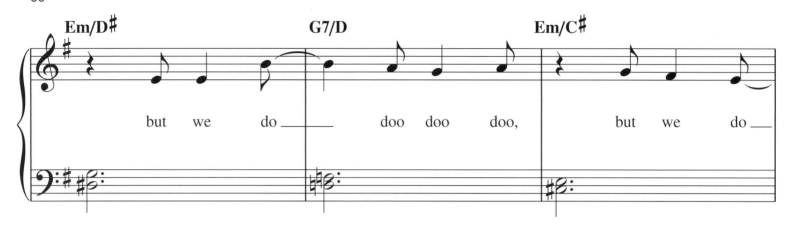

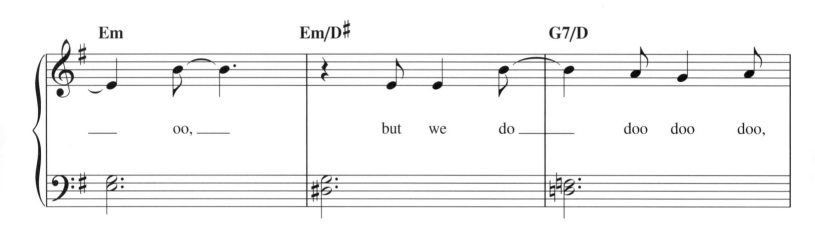

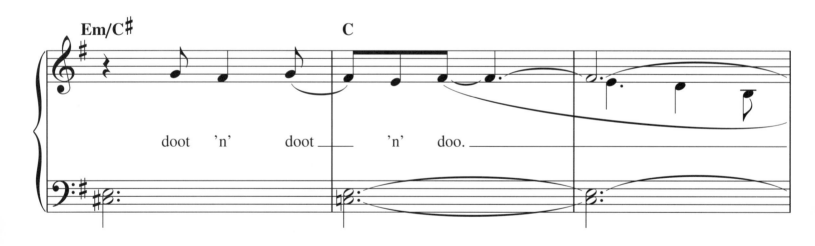

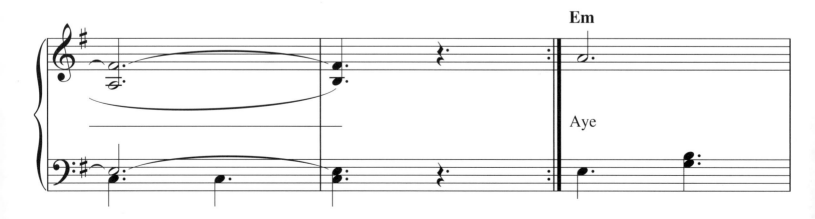

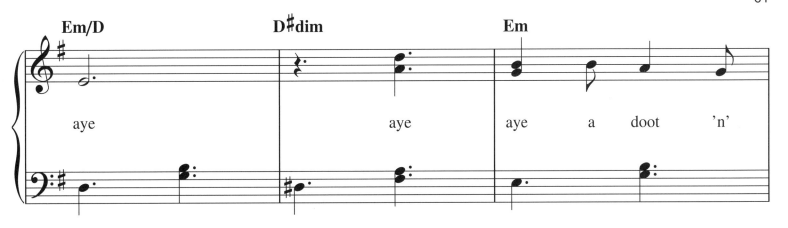

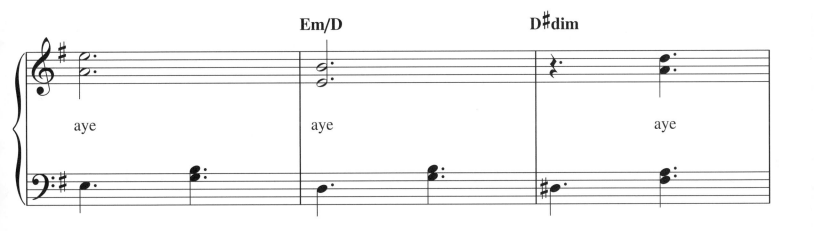

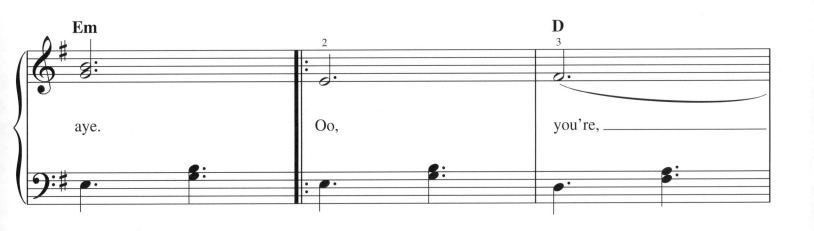

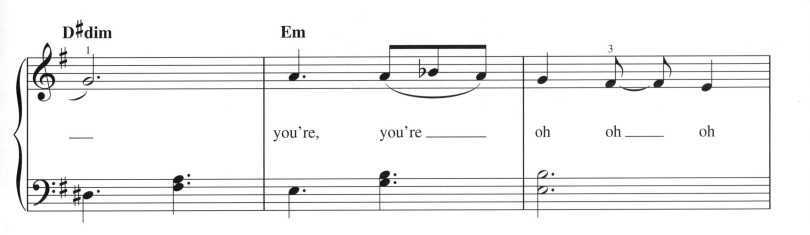

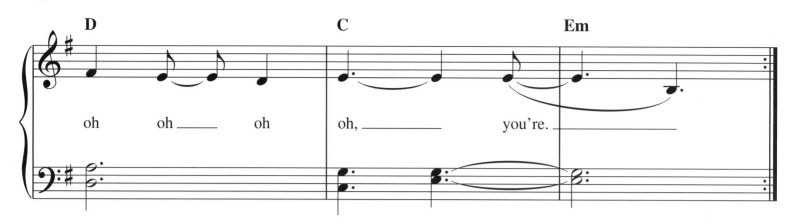

oh   oh ____ oh   oh, _____ you're. _____

Fa - vor - 'ti - sm   ain't ____   my   thing, ____   but ____
Fa - vor - 'ti - sm   ain't ____   my   thing, ____   but ____

____   in   the   sit - u - a - tion
____   I'd   be   glad   to   make   an

I'd   be ____   glad. ____
ex - cep - tion. ____   Whoa, _____

D.S. al Coda
(1st verse)

whoa.

CODA

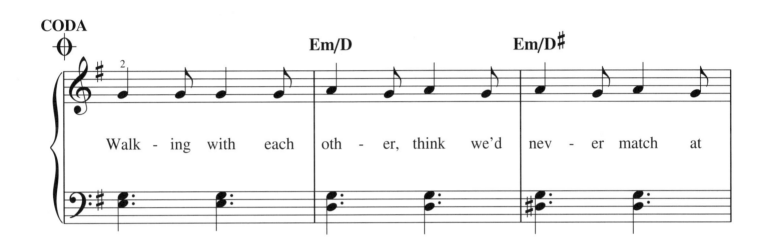

Em/D   Em/D#

Walk - ing with each oth - er, think we'd nev - er match at

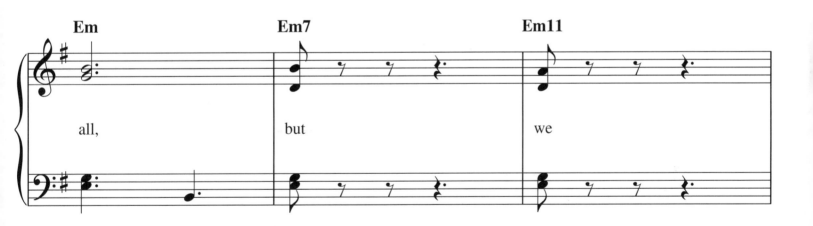

Em   Em7   Em11

all,   but   we

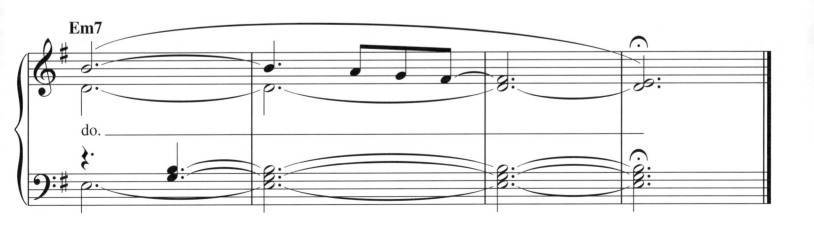

Em7

do.

TIRED

Words and Music by ADELE ADKINS
and FRANCIS EG WHITE

Moderately, in 2

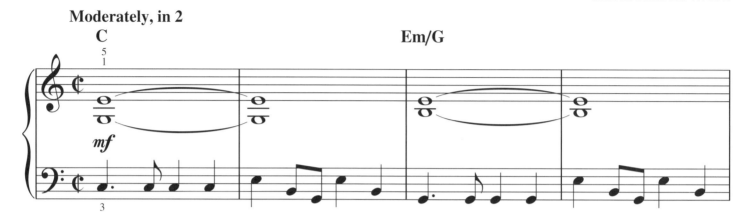

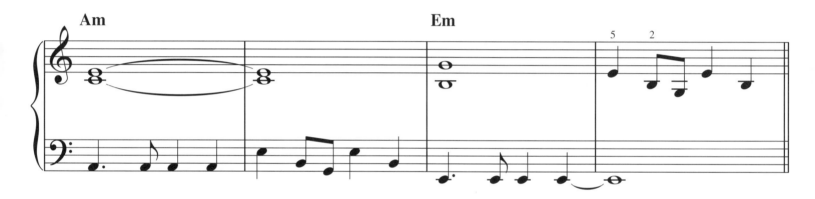

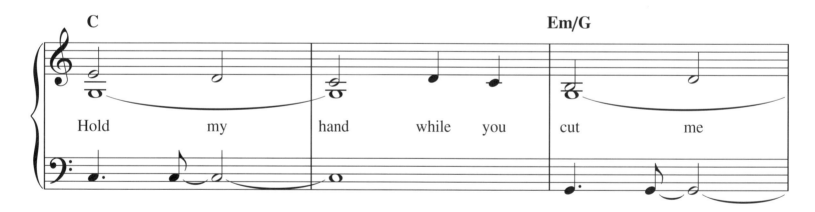

Hold   my   hand   while   you   cut   me

down.   It   had   on - ly   just   be - gun,   but   now   it's

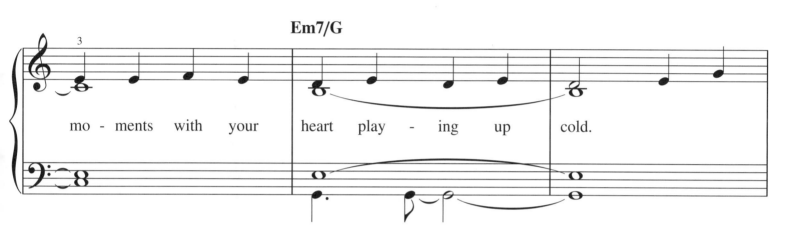

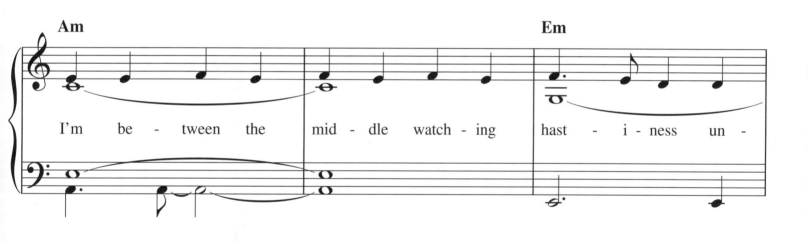

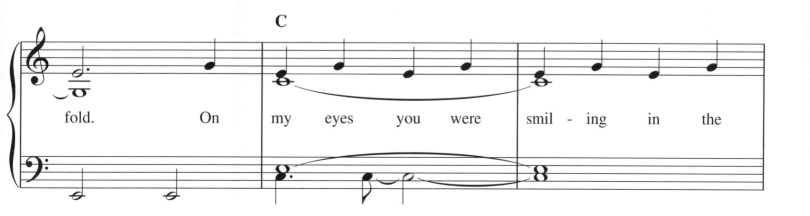

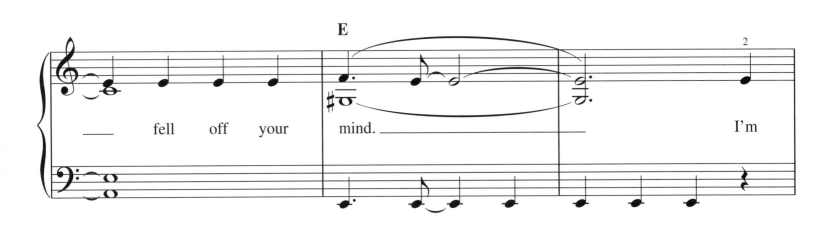

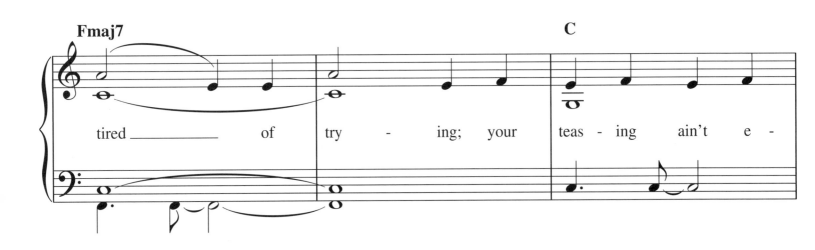

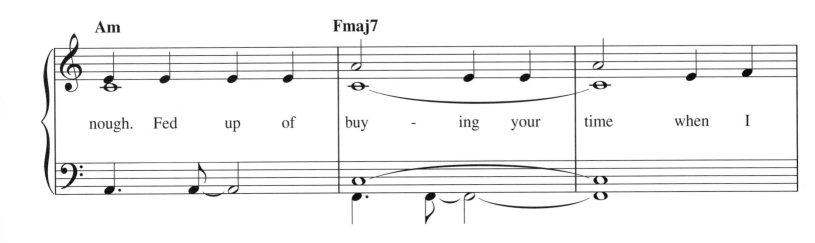

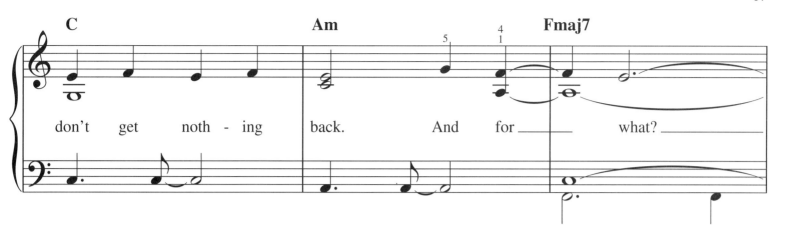

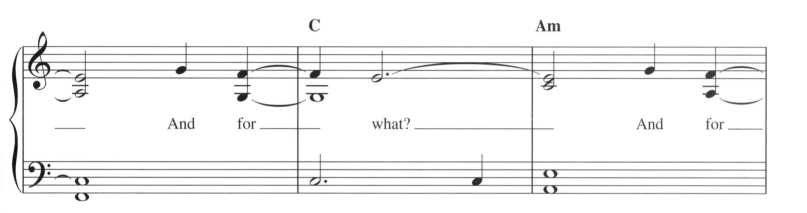

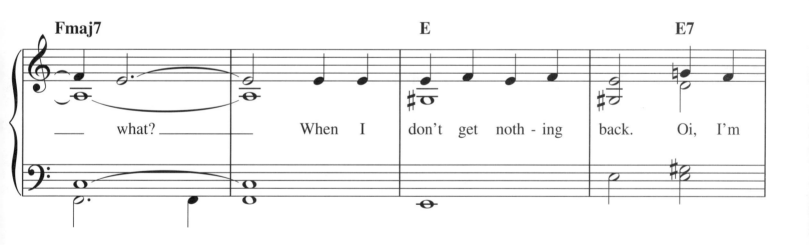

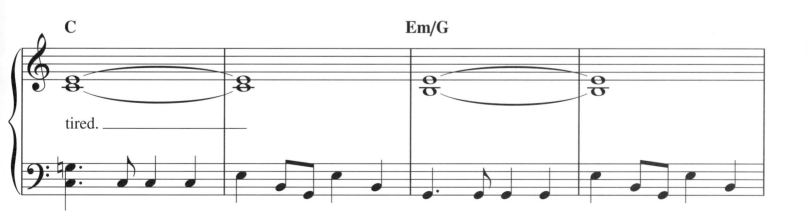

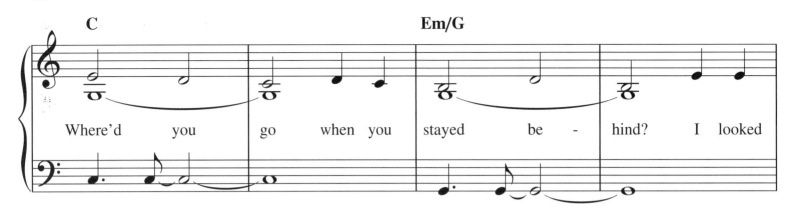

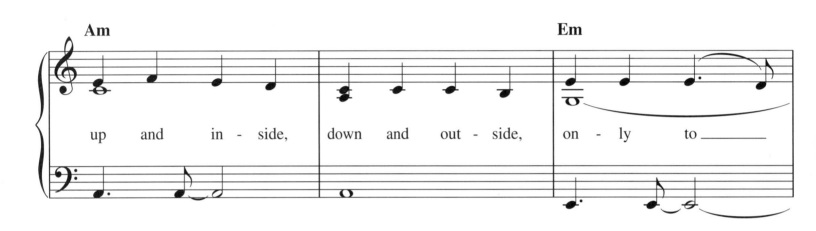

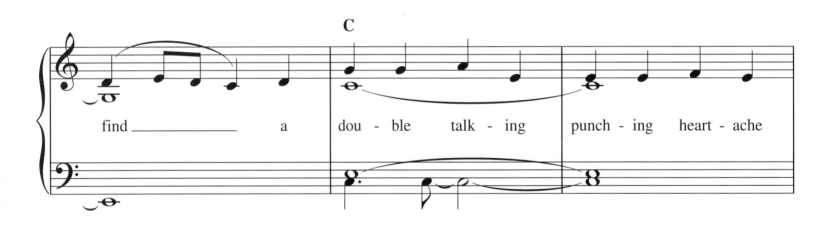

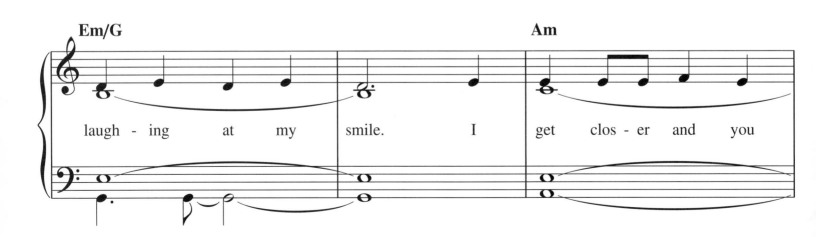

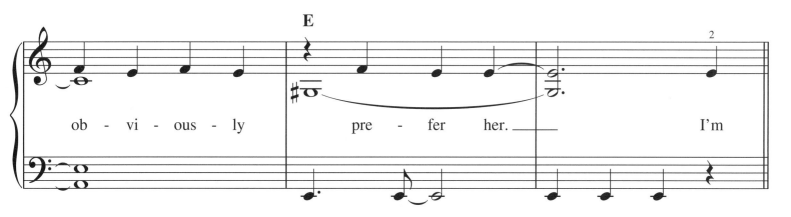

ob - vi - ous - ly pre - fer her. _____ I'm

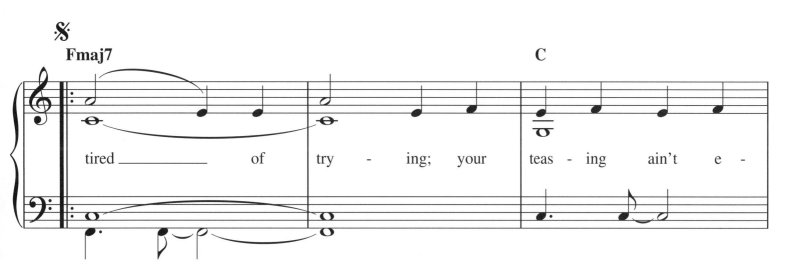

tired _____ of try - ing; your teas - ing ain't e -

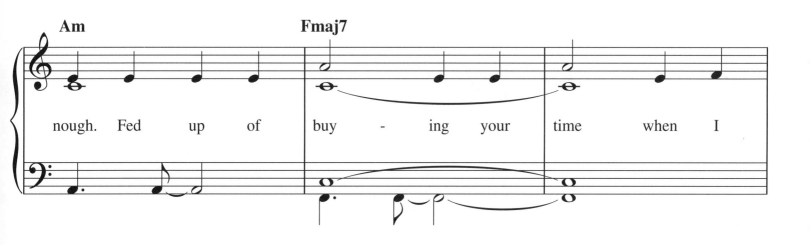

nough. Fed up of buy - ing your time when I

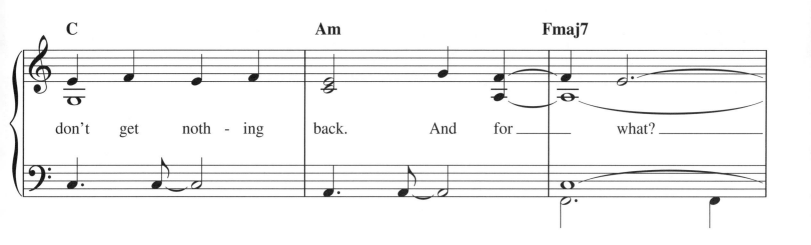

don't get noth - ing back. And for _____ what? _____

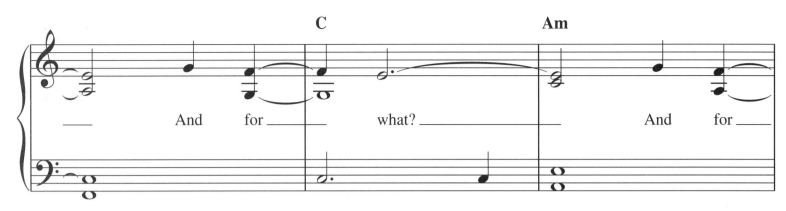

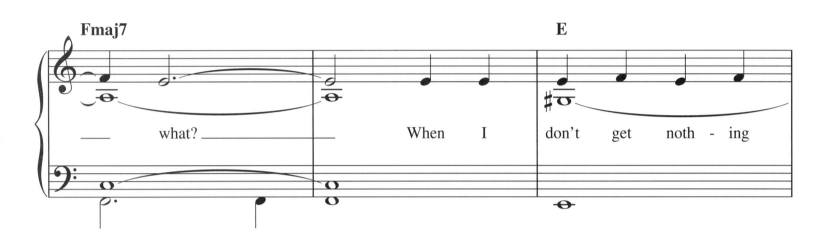

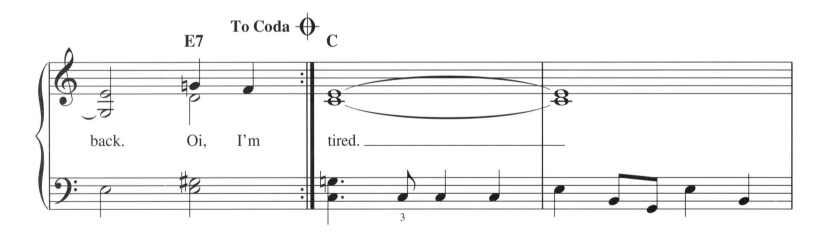

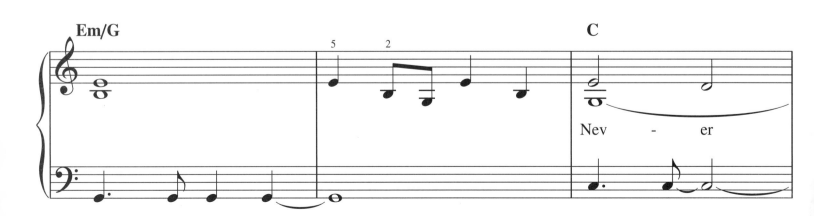

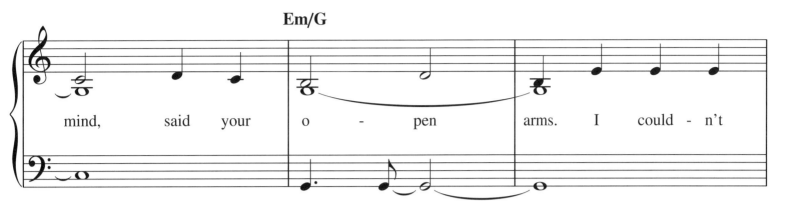

mind,   said   your   o - pen   arms.   I   could - n't

help   the   leap   that   tripped   me   back   in - to   them.   E -

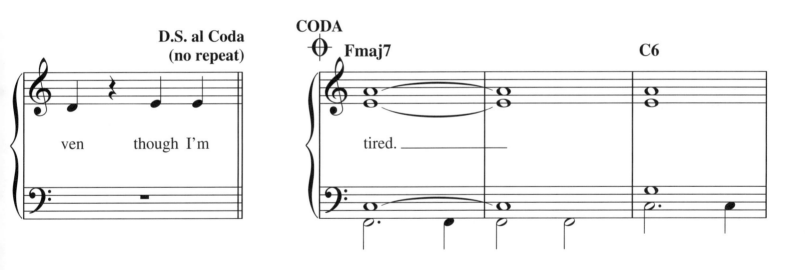

ven   though I'm   tired. _____

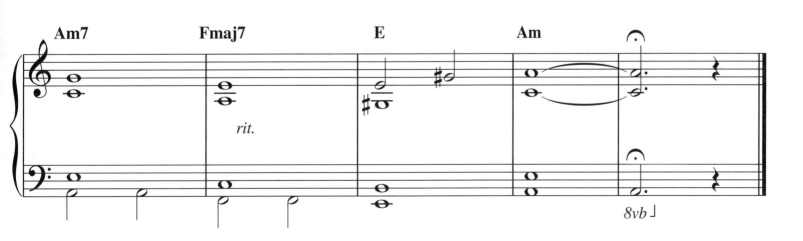

HOMETOWN GLORY

Words and Music by
ADELE ADKINS

Moderately, in 2

1. I've been walk-ing in the same way _
(2.) *See additional lyrics*

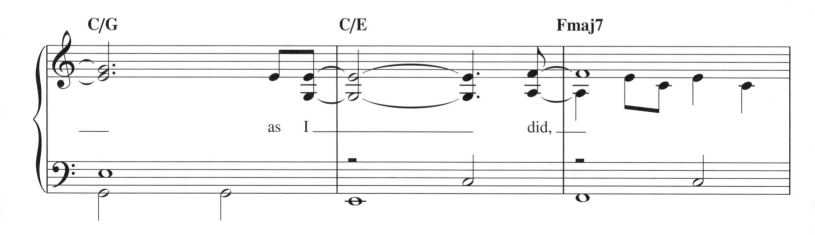

as I ___ did, ___

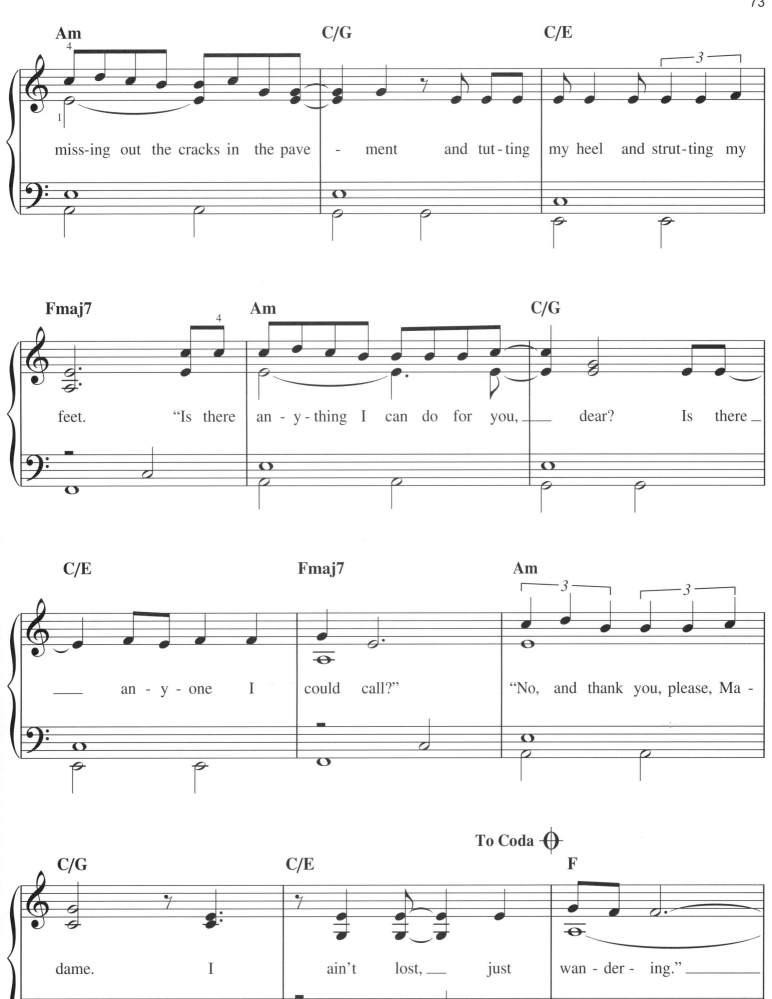

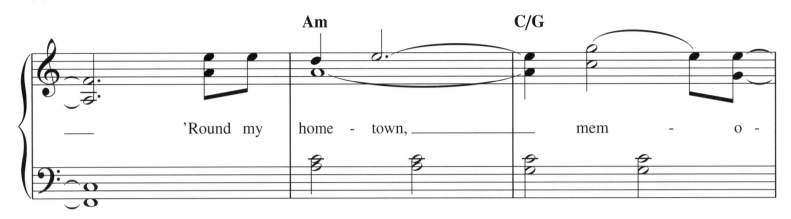

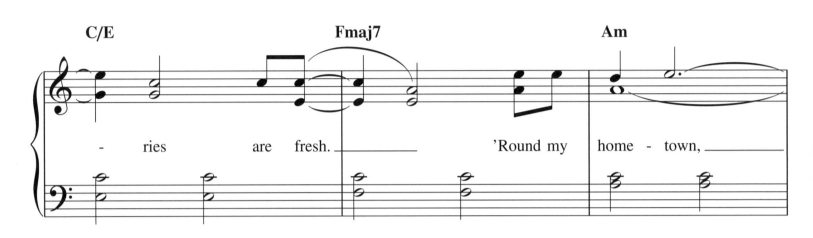

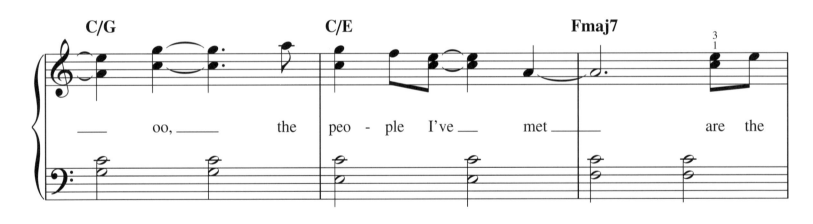

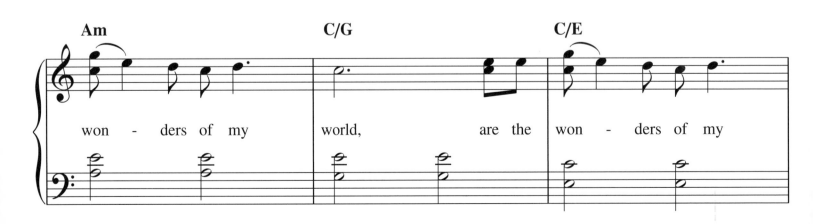

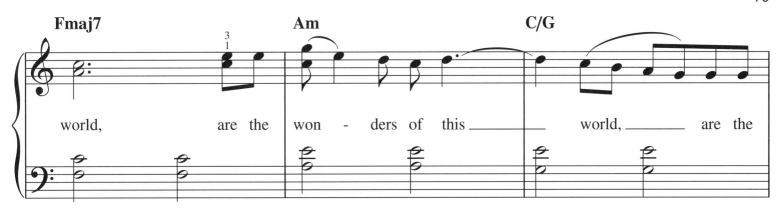

world,   are the   won - ders of this   world,   are the

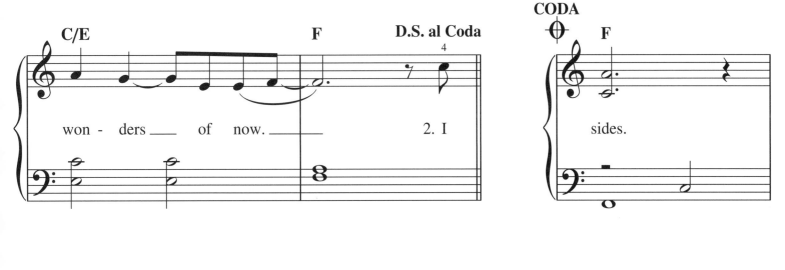

won - ders   of now.   2. I   sides.

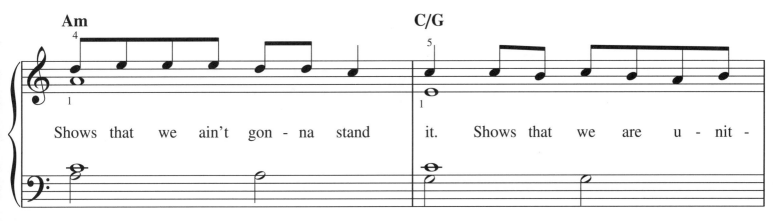

Shows that we ain't gon - na stand it. Shows that we are u - nit -

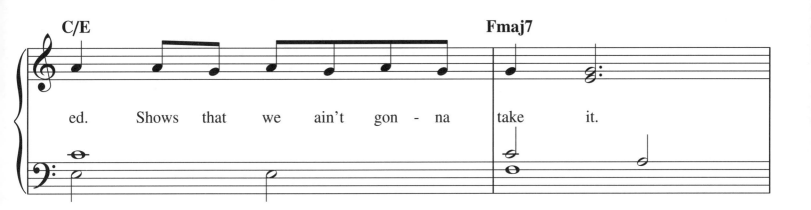

ed.   Shows that we ain't gon - na   take it.

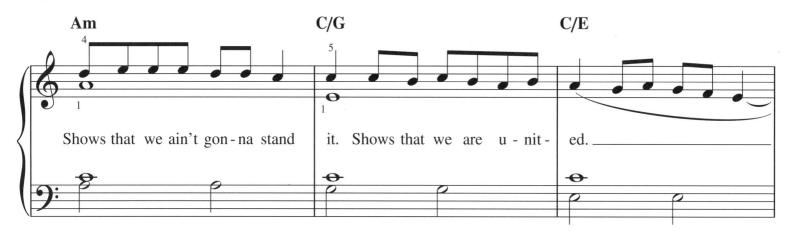

Shows that we ain't gon-na stand it. Shows that we are u-nit-ed. _____

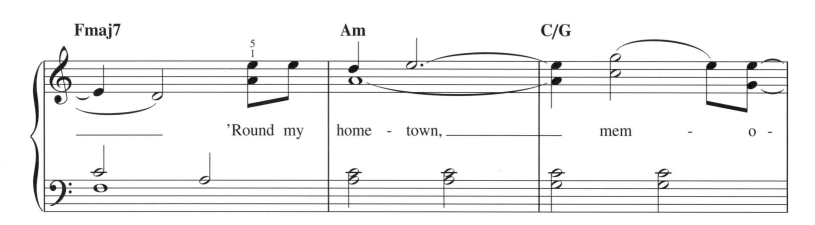

_____ 'Round my home-town, _____ mem - o -

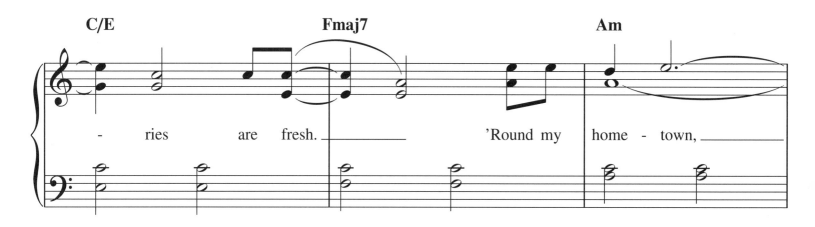

- ries are fresh. _____ 'Round my home-town, _____

__ oo, _____ the peo - ple I've ___ met _____ are the

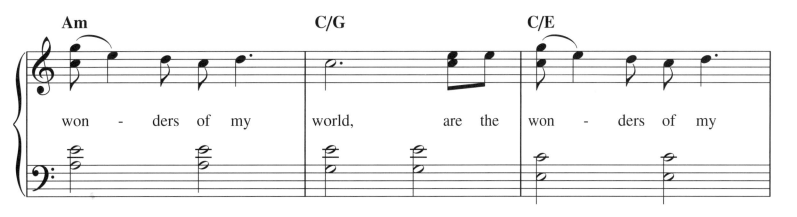

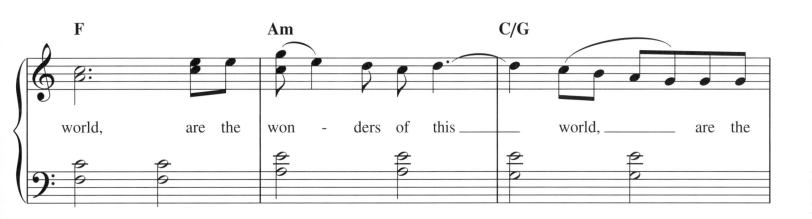

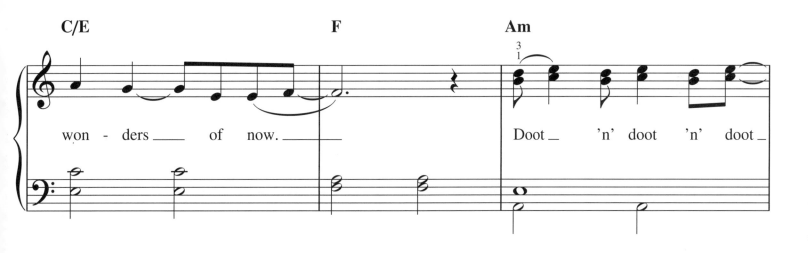

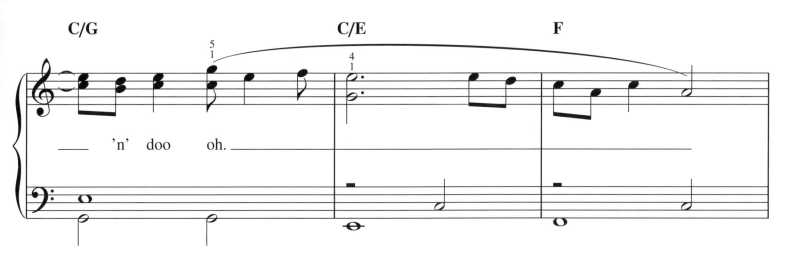

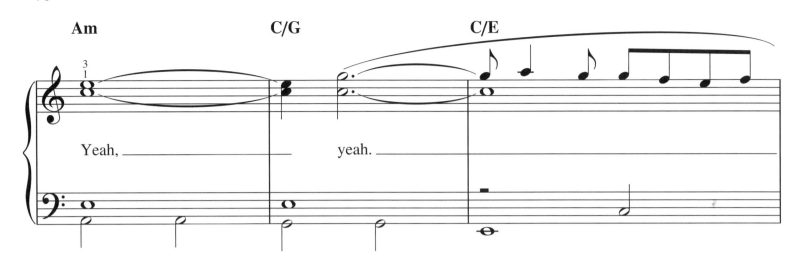

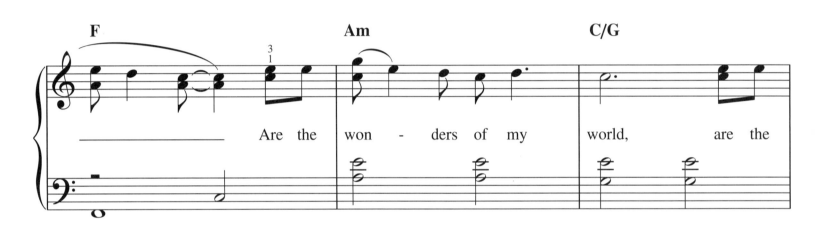

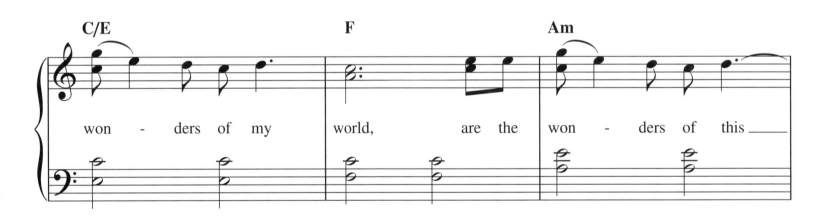

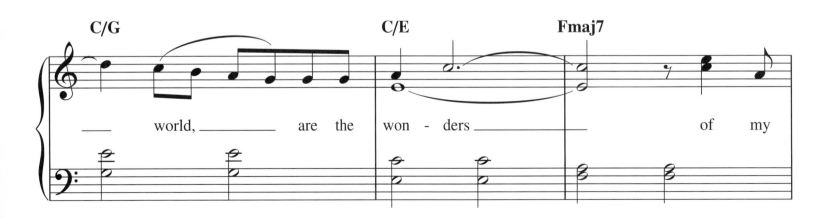

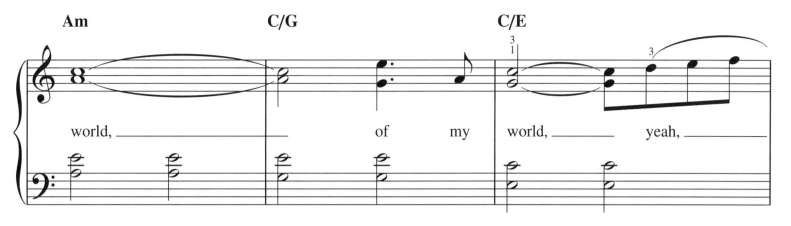

world, _____ of my world, _____ yeah, _____

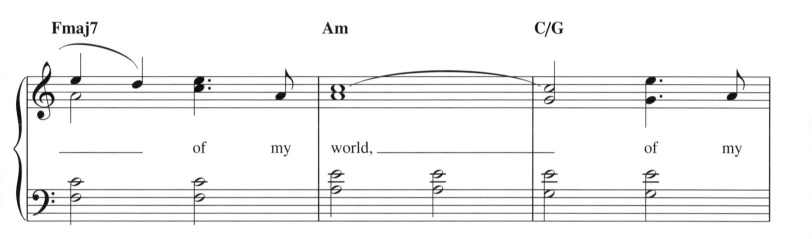

_____ of my world, _____ of my

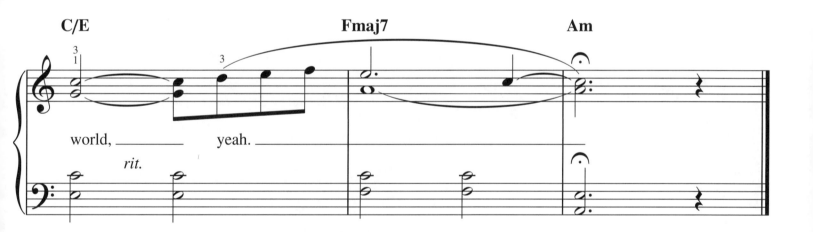

world, _____ yeah. _____
rit.

Additional Lyrics

2. I like it in the city when the air is so thick and opaque.
   I love seeing ev'rybody in short skirts, shorts and shades.
   I like it in the city when two worlds collide;
   You get the people in the government,
   Ev'rybody taking diff'rent sides. (To Coda)

   Shows that we ain't gonna stand it...